Garfield
Double Trouble

JIM DAVIS

D1637675

RR
RAVETTE PUBLISHING

First published by Ravette Publishing 1999

Printed and bound in Great Britain
for Ravette Publishing Limited,
Unit 3, Tristar Centre,
Star Road, Partridge Green,
West Sussex RH13 8RA
by Cox & Wyman Ltd, Reading, Berkshire

ISBN: 1 84161 008 9

FLING!

JIM DAVIS 7-23

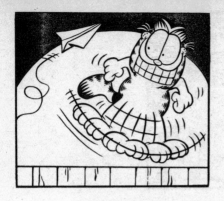

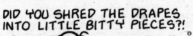

© 1996 PAWS, INC./Distributed by Universal Press Syndicate

SWAT

JIM DAVIS 9-11

GET OUT OF MY WAY!

JIM DAVYS 10-1

© 1996 PAWS, INC./Distributed by Universal Press Syndicate

© 1996 PAWS, INC./Distributed by Universal Press Syndicate

© 1996 PAWS, INC./Distributed by Universal Press Syndicate

© 1996 PAWS, INC./Distributed by Universal Press Syndicate

YOU'RE A LAZY PIG!

HOW DID HE KNOW IT WAS ME?

OTHER GARFIELD BOOKS AVAILABLE

Pocket Books @ £2.99 each	ISBN
Byte Me	1 84161 009 7
Flying High	1 85304 043 6
A Gift For You	1 85304 190 4
The Gladiator	1 85304 941 7
Going Places	1 85304 242 0
Great Impressions	1 85304 191 2
Hangs On	1 85304 784 8
Happy Landings	1 85304 105 X
Here We Go Again	0 948456 10 8
In The Pink	0 948456 67 1
In Training	1 85304 785 6
The Irresistible	1 85304 940 9
Just Good Friends	0 948456 68 X
Le Magnifique!	1 85304 243 9
Let's Party	1 85304 906 9
On The Right Track	1 85304 907 7
On Top Of The World	1 85304 104 1
Pick Of The Bunch	1 85304 258 7
The Reluctant Romeo	1 85304 391 5
Says It With Flowers	1 85304 316 8
Shove At First Sight	1 85304 990 5
Strikes Again	0 906710 62 6
To Eat, Or Not To Eat?	1 85304 991 3
Wave Rebel	1 85304 317 6
With Love From Me To You	1 85304 392 3

Theme Books @ £3.99 each	
Guide to Behaving Badly	1 85304 892 5
Guide to Creatures Great and Small	1 85304 998 0
Guide to Healthy Living	1 85304 972 7
Guide to Insults	1 85304 895 X
Guide to Pigging Out	1 85304 893 3
Guide to Romance	1 85304 894 1
Guide to The Seasons	1 85304 999 9
Guide to Successful Living	1 85304 973 5

Classics @ £4.99 each   ISBN
Volume One   1 85304 970 0
Volume Two   1 85304 971 9
Volume Three   1 85304 996 4
Volume Four   1 85304 997 2

Miscellaneous
Garfield Treasury   £9.99   1 85304 975 1

Garfield Address & Birthday   1 85304 918 2
Book Gift Set   £7.99 inc VAT

Garfield 21st Birthday   1 85304 995 6
Celebration Book   £9.99

All Garfield books are available at your local bookshop or from the address below.
Just tick the titles required and send the form with your payment to:-

B.B.C.S., P.O. BOX 941, HULL, NORTH HUMBERSIDE HU1 3YQ
24 Hour Telephone Credit Card Line 01482 224626
Prices and availability are subject to change without notice.
Please enclose a cheque or postal order made payable to B.B.C.S. to the value of
the cover price of the book and allow the following for postage and packing:

U.K. & B.F.P.O.:	£1.95 (weight up to 1kg)		3-day delivery
	£2.95 (weight up to 1kg up to 20kg)		3-day delivery
	£4.95 (weight up to 20kg)		next day delivery
EU & Eire:	Surface Mail	£2.50 for first book & £1.50 for subsequent books	
	Airmail	£4.00 for first book & £2.50 for subsequent books	
USA:	Surface Mail	£4.50 for first book & £2.50 for subsequent books	
	Airmail	£7.50 for first book & £3.50 for subsequent books	
Rest of	Surface Mail	£6.00 for first book & £3.50 for subsequent books	
The World:	Airmail	£10.00 for first book & £4.50 for subsequent books	

Name ....

Address ....

....

....

Cards accepted: Visa, Mastercard, Switch, Delta, American Express

Expiry Date ....Signature ....